Anti-Buddha

Dark Philosophy

2025 Edition

A.B
Antibooks Collection
CASSA Editions

Collection: Antibooks
Writer: A.B
Copyrighted text.
Last edited: February 2025
Images extracted from the web (Unknown authors)

ISBN: 9798312410587
Independently published

Independent publication
First edition date: 01/09/2019
By CASSA Editions

The chapters
1. Self-conception
2. Passion
3. Love
4. Unity
5. Balance
6. Life
7. Death
8. Vanity
9. Power
10. Obedience
11. Resistance
12. Freedom

Chapter 1
Self-conception

I'm not God, no.
But in my shadows, the divine darkness reigns.
With false modesty and honest reverence, I see myself candidly like a little monster.
No longer influenced by the light, I have approached the shadows by my own choice.

I had always been taught that light outshines darkness, just as wisdom surpasses ignorance.

But, was this truly so?

Over time, I came to view this belief as mistaken and audacious. A naive and painful illusion: to believe in the supremacy of light over shadow, of wisdom over ignorance, or of good over evil.

It all began in a moment, when I sought strength, when I vowed never to lie to myself again. Meditation then led me to the abyss, to the darkest depths of consciousness. There, I stripped bare the lies that surrounded me, and discovered that light, with its dazzle, did nothing but deceive. Whereas darkness, in its shadows, harbors a truth simpler and more authentic.

In somber introspection deep,
I find unreality and disillusion sweep.
Though mortal my condition stands,
I refuse the chains of illusive hands.
Darkness, in its stark honesty, has shown
That light teems with contradiction, overblown.
It is the root of all my joy and sorrow,
My poverty and wealth, the borrow.
For light plays a game of shadows and beams,
That is its craft, the fabric of its schemes.

The light, in which we humans place so much trust, had been blinding me with its falsehoods and illusions. It kept me captive in a seeming sense of clarity. Yet, it was in the darkness that I found truth, where I discovered redemption. Meditative silence, far from being empty, is a space filled with secrets and a portal to deeper truths that mere superficial reason cannot unveil. By releasing myself from the light, I understood the simple essence of existence. I discovered my true nature: ignorant, vibrant, dark.

Now, it feels like a delay to hear white tales and pretenses about the virtues of light. Associations with goodness and wisdom turn out to be suitable contradictions that the most dazzled repeat charmingly, like beautiful melodies whose lyrics are mere fictions.

For its part, darkness, which always seemed enigmatic to me, ceased to be nothingness. As the dwelling place of light, it revealed itself as an ocean of infinite possibilities and absolute revelations.

By descending into its depths, I was able to find true absolution and free myself from the chains of everyday existence.

Now, as I am shaped in the darkness, I feel the presence, the diligence, the vision, and the infinite, omnipotent breath that resides in my body; your body or our body. Freeing myself from the anxiety that disturbs humanity, I overcome the illusion of identity. Merging with the immaterial and eternal, I am to enter into the collective consciousness, spreading gently like a shadow that envelops everything.

Integration into the supreme nebulous state.

Dissolving force of all light.

Capturer of the space where time resides.

Darkness holds in its essence three cardinal powers:

The first: It can see through the illusions of the world, revealing its deceits.
The second: It is a dissolving force, capable of liberating all beings from their bonds.
And the third: It captures the energies of consciousness, facilitating the abandonment of any mind to a fully unconscious state.

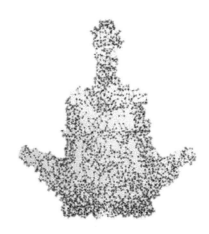

Now, the dark meditative spirit dwells in me and has found its purposes:
To show the true nature of the cosmos: immense, indifferent, and ambivalent.
To reveal the feat that only the dark immensity can offer: the total absolution of consciousness.

From the voice of the redeeming prophet, the eternal longing is as follows:
May the deep silence envelop us,
May darkness purify us,
And may the eternal emptiness guide and relieve us.

Given my context, I cannot claim to be a transcendental being who has understood reality and become an enlightened one. To say that would be little more than falling into another illusion woven by light.

The word Buddha is often a title or epithet and sometimes a name. It means "one who is awake" in the sense of having awakened to reality. In that regard, the light gave me the key to name myself.

I, who seek the opposite of that being, having reversed the goal of meditation, seeking not enlightenment but a return to the dark dream, tend to think of myself as The Antibuddha.

Chapter 2
Passion

Countless perceptions conjecture that the opposite of love is hate. Yet, at the same time, there are discernments suspecting that they are two sides of the same coin. The coin is passion, and its value is illusory. Only with irradiation can we deceive ourselves and believe that we are experiencing it.

The mind becomes adept at the tricks of light and the spells of passion, seeking good despite not knowing how to extend it, automatically battling evil without knowing how to suppress it, professing love and condemning hate. Passion clouds our vision.

    Neither good do we understand, nor evil do we comprehend.

In weakness: we love one another. While in strength: we compete and despise. Passion stirs us and holds us at its mercy, suffering impiety and enjoying reward, despite being two steps of the same path and two sides of the same coin.

                        Passion stirs us and binds us.

Obedient to an idea considered master, we resist meditation or our own contemplation; passion takes away our mental independence and makes us malleable and doctrinable. Whoever charms our energies moves us without much effort.

                                          Passion plays us.

Passion makes us pleasurably small, allowing us to delve and move within a small cage where everything that excites us resides. When passion reigns in the mind, the beings living within us reflect filth, zeal, and ego.

Exaltations blind us to the pettiness of our being, yet our behavior in the eyes of meditation appears grasping and self-interested; miserly with ideas that suit us; sordid with ideas foreign to our passion; selective and accommodating to opinions that decorate us; and mocking towards new ideas that disrupt the preservation of our adorations.

Passion guards.

By reflection, tranquility is the true opposite of passion and love or hate. Similar opposites are calm to exaltation, restraint to impetus, coldness to inflaming or restraint to frenzy. All adversaries of passion can be managed through the act of meditation, which is a way to develop mental states characterized by serenity, concentration, awareness, equanimity, and balance.

       Meditation freezes passion.

When meditation puts passion under its lens, the teachings that are reached arrive at the fields of self-control, to the mountains of carefreeness, to the heights of coldness, the lakes of power, the forests of libertinage, to the plains of measure, to the cities of madness, and to the great palaces where the lie of ethics inhabits.

Everything is uncovered through meditation.

Examining the character that contrasts with one driven by passion, we encounter an individual who transcends all doctrines. This person is unable to adhere to a singular guiding principle and is open to embracing new ideas that may challenge existing beliefs. They embody a state of meditation unclouded by convenience, zeal, or ego, achieving a remarkably empty and pure mental state. Such a state is invaluable for comprehending and observing phenomena without imposing a subjective lens. This introspective mind practices isolation, intentionally refraining from any distractions beyond the event being observed. It is this mind that can recreate an event in its most natural form, uncovering the underlying forces through reflective insight that clarifies and reveals the intentions at play.

The meditator is not the plaything of passion.

Meditation allows our dark will to delve into the hallways of mental libraries where anti-philosophical lessons and studies of human vanity are visible in all its aspects: intellectual, emotional, spiritual, and cultural.

The mind is more vain than philosophical.

Passion stirs the soul while meditation observes,
Passion acts relentless, as meditation draws its curves.
Passion builds ideas, while meditation takes apart,
Passion chases stimuli, while meditation follows the heart.

Chapter 3
Love

Love is the kind of energy that can exhilarate and brighten the soul. From the beginning of their lives, many beings grow accustomed to it. The energy with which mothers embrace their offspring to impart comfort, stability, and refuge is rightly called love. From there, it is evident that love's primary function is to create an environment conducive to the positive development of life.

Love is by nature a desired stimulus.

But love is not merely harmony, peace, or positive development. I would be ashamed of myself if I were not reflective enough to distinguish between generous actions and the tricks and plagues that come with love. Those who ponder this can understand that sometimes the tricks and good deeds are so homogeneously mixed that the application of love generates as many bad consequences, if not more, than good ones.

Love is double-edged.

And although, in practice, love brings many plagues and generates many evident evils, to point it out and accuse it of being impious, dirty, and dishonest is undoubtedly a tough and unrepentant task.

    Judging love is the bravest audacity.

The Judgment of Love

It is a stoic act of arresting the conscience to pinpoint both the virtues and vices in the practice of love. Given that these values are interpreted uniquely by each individual, the challenge of assessing them multiplies infinitely. Nevertheless, the prevailing consensus is that "love" embodies affection, understanding, empathy, respect, and aiding others. From this, we discern that the word "love" attains an almost sacred status.

The Virtues of Love

Life, liberty, and harmony.

It is said that love brings peace, nurtures generosity, advances humanity, and aligns with a series of well-intentioned actions that foster the wholesome development of beings, their families, and their friends. Thus, it is believed that love secures life, liberty, and imparts a sense of harmony.

The Capacity to Forgive
Another virtue of love is the capacity to forgive. It is expected that a loving person can empathize and absolve faults, transcending the selfishness that often incites conflicts.

Optimism
Optimism is another benign element that forms an integral part of love. Since forgiving involves the desire to move forward, and moving forward is the essential trait of optimism, it follows that a central characteristic of love is optimism.

Its virtues are clear and beyond reproach, yet its afflictions devour all its merits.

The "plagues" of love

All the virtues of love fall or decompose due to the plagues it brings with it. It is easy for its well-intentioned actions to deform and mislead due to our errant minds that have never acquired a real understanding of the meaning of the word. Love filled with selfish interests is constantly practiced by those of us who are apathetic and overprotected. And thus, we conform the perverse social system in which we are immersed. Some of us are the ruins of love and are completely indifferent to its authentic meaning.

Overprotection

In love comes an enduring embrace of protection. And among the acts of pampering and affection, a delicate sense of belonging is nurtured.

These elements are dangerous principles of egocentrism, hoarding, ingratitude, and some other vile actions laden with more ferocity.

Egoism

Those of us who poorly execute or do not properly conceive the agreement of the concept of love are many, and the way we practice this energy is filled with numerous selfish tricks that cause the constant war in this world. This is recalled when looking at protectionism, alienation, jealousy;

which are the most common plagues of love and give rise to more vile feelings such as envy, greed, resentment, and even hate, which is the other side of the passionate coin where the aforementioned love is found.

Apathy

Authentic love should not be problematic; however, corrupt love is. Love that is not well cultivated or poorly learned will come accompanied by tricks and malice that go against its main purpose: to promote an empathetic attitude and shelter the human condition, which is vulnerable to abuse of power.

Its vices are evident, but still, the courage to turn around and face them is not enough.

The murky root of a clean love

It is not out of joy that love is poorly crafted and poorly consumed by our addicted and inattentive people. However, upon reviewing how the alliance of the word "love" arises socially, we locate that its most real sense carries a darker and murkier origin. True, pure love without curses exists, but it is mostly in the consciousness of beings who have suffered the ravages and misfortunes caused by the plagues of its predecessor: corrupt, unrestrained, and unruly love.

The purest love manages to arise from a murky root, from a black origin, from a horrifying past. The need to repair the ruins and misfortunes of uncontrolled love, and the precision to establish a cleaner love as a necessary atmosphere for peace are understandings that arise in beings trampled and spiritually stuffed by abuses of power.

That unbridled, crazed, cursed love; as it is practiced in society, painfully impacts the gnosis of more and more consciousnesses, and these manage to understand the fragile and delicate condition of our individual bodies and minds. In reaction to this misfortune, their understanding creates the delicate social intentionality of practicing a purer and clearer love, of giving what one wishes to receive, of truly providing a majestic title to the word and purifying it of all its plagues.

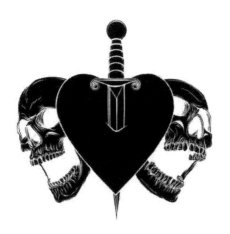

The only way to make conscience see, is to tear its heart.

Condemned Souls

Those souls that have not spiritually freed themselves from the disorders of abuse are the ones who, without any conscience or consideration, have committed and will commit more atrocities and injustices that will lead to new affected consciousnesses being prone to soften and give themselves a more real understanding of the meaning of love.

> Some souls cause evil
> so that others understand goodness.

The souls whose gnosis softens in reaction to the ravages of abuse and violence become truly loving beings. In contrast, the condemned souls are distinguished by reacting with hardness and anger to the same circumstances, demonstrating that they are still possessed by their selfishness and that their sense of justice revolves only around themselves.

On the other hand, liberated spirits see beyond themselves; their attitude is filled with optimism and absolution, and their understanding of justice is broader. The loving will want to unite and support others to guide their actions toward an empathetic social intentionality.

> The justice of loving spirits only grows when
> they eradicate their own evil.

Forgiveness and empathy are personal values that arise in beings who have understood their fragile and imperfect condition, delicate beings who have been strengthened by love. Those who have not been properly revitalized by this energy cannot forgive or empathize.

Love without plagues is only a guest in the houses with consciousness of their fragile and delicate condition.

While some people progress in the meaning of love, the abuse of power continues to cause disturbances that feed hatred, resentment, and other impure feelings in other people.

Overlooking that they will further deteriorate their consciousness, these people will try to fight against injustice in their own deranged way: hostile uprisings, furious calls for attention, and other acts of rebellion and disturbance to make themselves heard.

Deranged individuals fight to overcome injustice when the only justice is to cleanse love.

Disturbed beings with chaotic revenge inevitably emerge in the social system time and again because if liberated souls absolve the intolerable, the crazed souls think they must make themselves heard.

And with anarchy, attention is called for in a dizzying manner. This call for attention seeks understanding, but the social nature reacts whimsically; it causes chaotic and violent forces, instead of finding understanding, to find opposition. Thus, the lost souls suffer the bitterness of a frustrated search. Again, and again.
A violent reaction seeks understanding, but always finds disapproval.

The deceptions mixed in love promote the growth of abuse of power in an increasingly filthy society. And while the most egocentric practice mistreatment of consciousness through rebellious acts, the beings aware of their fragile condition become more necessary and precise on the stage; because if the maniacs continue fighting and further deteriorating the environment, only the understanding ones will be able to stop them.
Only understanding extinguishes the fire of disputes.

From the source of true love, waters of understanding and care flow to irrigate the strength of empathy. Due to the fragility and delicacy of the individual condition, free souls will understand that they must work together to strengthen themselves.

After putting love under the lens of meditation, we understand that we cannot place ourselves before it. And we comprehend that it is not love that decomposes the world but the deception attached to it and the misunderstanding of its concept. Finally, we end up doing the only thing that meditation can do: achieve disillusionment. And even with all that the lens of reflection reveals to us: We are left to vent the question: How do we feel about all this?

In the present time, when observing the true loving acts of people, we see that they have decided to support themselves through a cordial and helpful attitude. The social intention called "love" gradually harbors human weaknesses and tries to make this refuge its strength. However, hypocrisy and false love grow in tandem, and humanity remains in a midpoint between honesty and corruption; carrying out actions both courteous and cruel, conducting their morality with half honesty and half impunity; living and dying in a place between dignity and humiliation.

Personally, I chose to understand strength to then return to unconsciousness. I have decided to become a dark and impassive being. My main motivation is to see others strengthen with true love, and my inaction will reside in letting them see their imperfect condition for themselves, even if it takes an eternity.

To inspire the gnosis of the filth they call love, I have already outlined some descriptions that haunt them, even if I myself become committed and dirty in the act. I choose to allow the painful lessons that will tear and divide their consciousness, even if that does not please them. I surrender to the passion of battles, as long as they eventually achieve the dissolution of the roar, the ego, and jealousy.

Love is virtue, and it is desirable that every being understands its true meaning to strengthen us all. As for my present spirit, momentarily I cannot strengthen it with this energy knowing that it is full of plagues and lies. So, I choose unconsciousness, immutability; I choose to expand darkness. Our true strength will be meditation and thus, the total understanding of strength.

In a world full of filth, with meditation we can transmute everything.

Chapter 4
Unity

Unity is achieved when agreements are forged among multiple individuals, entities, or groups, centered around a common purpose, concern, and mutual benefit.
                                        Unity is an arrangement.

Unity is a dream realized, a fulfillment that arrives with the consolidation of elements that enable the functions and arrangements birthed by the union.
                   Illusion, figuration, disposition, and unity.

Those who open their doors and provide others with the resources that a changing time and space allow them to possess undoubtedly think of creating unity with other beings.

Sharing resources and responsibilities are the foundational visions of unity's dreamers.

The envisioned unity, the direct object of dreamers' fantasies, is initially simulated, distinct yet invariably varied by the subjectivity of each dreamer.

The envisioned unity is first imagined by each individual.

It is concluded that unity is the pathway to coexistence. Unity sanctions agreements, agreements enable the formation of a system, and the system offers services to its components by its own members.

Arrangements are systematized within a unity.

The command of one or another system is established by some master idea, which is protected by the components or members of the system by the strength of the agreement. The devotion of the members to this master idea reinforces the minds that design how the system works.

The master persuades the unity, and the unity propels the master idea.

The complete compliance of the system's members and its smooth operation engender the sensation known as harmony. When a system is in harmony, it is prone to expansion due to the absence of opposing forces. This leads to what is known as the feedback of energy, an intensification of dynamism that will cease due to the enigmatic forces of balance. For everything that grows unchecked tends towards an eventual burst.

And ultimately, we will observe how the forces of balance challenge harmony.

Chapter 5
Balance

Destruction has a negative role concerning creation, but it is part of balance. In this spatiality that I scrutinize thought with thought, I can notice that harmony is the unity that destroys itself.

Spatiality always has a bipolar force; the ambivalence of the cosmos never stops spinning.

This bipolar force is adept at dividing and multiplying its infinite energy time and again. It complicates everything, yet gradually it constructs coherence. As it multiplies, a cohesion and a deeper understanding of the multiplicity of beings emerge.

Simple things complicate everything, and all complex things simplify into knowledge.

As it creates, it also destroys. As it complicates, it synthesizes. As it expands, it contracts. The bipolar force stretches and tightens; in diminishment, it rests; in extinction, it bursts forth and revives.

Balance is a force of many poles,
Ever-present, silent in its roles.
Whether noted or unseen,
It binds us tight, will not let us flee.

It cannot forever end what exists.
There will always be something, and there will never be nothing.
Mortals and immortals
In balance forever and ever.

Chapter 6
Life

Life finally reveals itself to me as it is, an irradiation of light, multiple in its forms, diverse in its games, and always consciously unconscious.

Consciousness is only something,
unconsciousness is everything.
Consciousness can be much or little;
unconsciousness can be the whole or it can be
nothing.

If there is sadness in consciousness,
in unconsciousness there is forgetfulness.
If there is misery in consciousness,
in unconsciousness there is wealth.
If there is guilt in consciousness,
in unconsciousness there is absolution.
If in consciousness there is any conflict,
in unconsciousness there is the solution.

Life is the maximum materiality we have until we dismantle the individual. Then a god is born from unconsciousness, and here we are. Since we were born, we are everything; we no longer seek the light; we have transformed into it and seek darkness to live in it.

On permanence

Every form of matter that retains memory and self-will harbors a "dark interior."
> (A dark interior = a consciousness)

Life has learned to remain dormant in the darkness, which allows it to maintain "dark interiors" through the new days.
> (Consciousnesses sleep at night. They rest in darkness, and this enables us to give them a certain permanence through the days.)

Through this way of extending the existence of dark interiors, across intervals of light and darkness, life expresses itself in various forms and has gathered them in the same space-time we now call a planet.
> (Resting in periods of darkness and existing in periods of light, thousands of life forms have been created and assembled in one place that our human consciousness now calls the world.)

On the Meaning and Renewal of Dark Interiors

- Ignorance preserves the life of the "dark interiors"; the duration of their ignorance equals the lifespan of their lives.

> (Consciousnesses are naturally ignorant; when they cease to be ignorant, they cease to be consciousnesses.)

- The interaction between the luminous exterior and a dark interior is called existence.
> (Light gives space to time.)

- Space is formed by "luminous objects." And their "dark interiors" connect time.
> (Everything the eye perceives is space, but its dark consciousness creates time.)

- Everything that occupies a place in the same space is at the same time a luminous exterior and a dark interior. This is the ambivalence of existence.
> (The existence of beings has two values: matter and consciousness.)

- The reproduction of "dark interiors" generates multiple senses of life, and with their death, sustenance is given to their renewable existences.

(When consciousnesses die,
they return to the luminous exterior.
When consciousnesses are born,
they renew their dark interiors.)

- The cult and devotion to life germinate in each new consciousness thanks to the astonishment generated by its state of inexperience and incomprehension.
(The existential motivation of each consciousness springs from the shock to its mystery.)

In the human form, our current condition, we have often venerated magic, for it casts a certain spell of direction, devotion, and worship of our existence. However, now we worship the myopic sciences more fervently because perhaps we are seeking to end our beliefs.

By the power of our luminous energy, I sense that humanity could end its existence by opposing the forces of balance. In wanting to tyrannize all science, we might oppress our own presence. In wanting to subdue all behavior, we might diminish any feeling. In wanting to control everything, we might end up exploding everything. But this should not happen if we humans procure a good superstition, if we start a new religion.

After meditating unconsciously on the real place of individuals and their dark minds, I understood that those who seek inner enlightenment are confronting their individual annihilation in life. But only after understanding the self-destruction of their ego will they discern that they can be part of a whole god.

From the depths of my dark interior, I believe it is better to fan the magic than science, as magic is beautiful and mystical; it is exciting to know that there is a mysterious power within the darkness of every object in space. Because every exterior that absorbs and reflects light is also a being of dark interior, with whose power I may not yet have connected.

> Magic gives religion and sustenance to my current life.

Science can be exciting, revealing, and a giver of new powers. But if it does not come accompanied by a divine belief, faith in a supreme dark consciousness, then it will be the end for those who practice it.

> Science ends with the unknown, but it is shortsighted and lacks meaning.

Science bereft of God begins the dull,
Then spirals into despair, and eyes behold
The void in actions, meaning stripped and null.
A life enchants when roots are left untold.
We bury deep its mystery to reign,
To flourish life, exist without a trace,
Asleep we stay, in dreams we must remain,
Let consciousness and shadow interlace.
If science offers power vast and stark,
To darkness, mesmerized, we must return.
Within the mists, the sacred god we mark,
His creations vast we gaze and learn.
Behold, still shrouded in your essence rare,
Question, should your eyes unveil—
dare not!
In darkness lies the magic, rich and fair,
Embrace the night, where true enchantments wrought.

When you wake up everything ends
That is the total enlightenment
The truth is that there is no supreme
consciousness, only games and temporary senses.
Therefore, I surrender to the nebulosity.
Darkness is the only light that it's worth to spread.
The kingdom of sleep, the current world,
the eternal rest,
It will never finish
But it always ends.

Chapter 7
Death

Death is life's counterpart; both function because the other is always there. For life, death is the opportunity for renewal, for change, for killing boredom. For death, life is everything and yet nothing.

Understanding this, I realize that death is another way of saying "end." From what life might say about death, and the fear it instills in the dark interiors, it would be: "end." The word "end" is not absolute, yet it is the shock of all fears. Fear always fears an end, although not all ends are feared.

> Death and endings are cyclical, sometimes desired, other times feared.

The end is the origin of all fears, although there are those who think they fear a beginning, they actually fear the end of something established: their stability, their freedom, their career, their pride, their ideas, their love, their joy, their bodily comfort, their emotional well-being, or their very lives.

Thus, fear is a brake that must avoid reaching some unwanted end. Fear prevents or delays events, has its own force, and lives in the minds of both the protected and the unprotected.

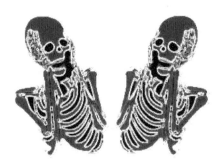

Fear possesses potential forces capable of evading meditation, concentration, and reflection, forces capable of clouding judgment and engrossing the self-centered mind. For our egocentric mind, the worst torment is the fear of its own death.

Death is nothing if we never had anything. Because nothing can end what never was. But if something ended, and that something hurt, then it indeed existed, perhaps unrecognized, but it was there.

Mourning

When grief is undeniable, the lost is not accepted, it is not let go. Grief is not overcome until one has decided to lose.

The tears of acceptance

When our mind falls into lamentation and tears emanate from our eyes, our emotional body is subjected to a process of confrontation with a certain loss and a certain pain.

The process of emotional acceptance is an important element in the dark origin of the purest love. For the weakness within the soul that cries will eventually forgive the event that afflicts it. Acceptance allows forgetting the misfortune, repairing the pain, and moving forward.

Sadness is the slow and painful acceptance of an event.

My eternal sense tells me that no living being, however perfect it may maintain itself, would want to be the same individual forever. Perhaps this is why we age, perhaps why we are vulnerable. Everything becomes more beautiful when we know that consciousness, however painful and pleasurable, is a journey we will eventually complete.

Eternal darkness brings new players to the game of life.

In the realm of darkness,
Light spells demise.
At any moment we might open our eyes,
And end the dream where comfort lies.
Yet we realize, amidst daily strife,
After a pause, our other life
Resumes with more continuity,
Part of a longer memory.

Our dreams, like little lives unfold,
Tiny tales that we behold,
Brief individual spans that lace
Into a broader, enduring trace.

Chapter 8
Vanity

Vanity is the seasoning of bodily existence, the sufficiency of mental presence, the fantasy of the soul, the pride of free will. Vanity is the boasting of calculation, the presumption of ideas, the vainglory of self-design.
      Presumption, boasting, vainglory, vanity.

Motivation and confrontation

The motivation each individual chooses for their existence may be in the interest of personal freedom or may be the preference for a mechanism to which they are duty-bound; from either impulse, confrontation with other wills and mechanisms becomes imminent.

> Individuals cling to their motivations, and their motivations give rise to their confrontations.

In any space where freedom resides, it is normal to encounter multiple confrontations of motives and meanings.

> Motive against motive. Meaning against meaning. Vanity against vanity.

Union and struggle of vanities

Those who share a presumption about the same subject often unite or clash. Factions are formed and face each other to win approval for their movement. The criterion of "the masses" swings from one side to another, always depending on the presentation of reasons. Individuals will lend their support to the side that can best demonstrate the justice of their cause.

What is justice, a consensus?

Justice must fit with the agreements of the crowd and the vanity that best suits the concerns of the era.

Justice = Popular pride.

Human justice is the accumulation of agreements from an era that are instituted and marked to watch over the convenience of the social system.
But in which era could human justice go beyond the convenience of its own species?

Contemporary social justice breeds, supports, and shields the egocentrism of individuals privileged by its protectionist policies, regardless of the condition of disadvantaged beings affected by the human race's economic system.

What we call human justice, is it egocentrism?

Egocentrism and vanity are attitudes that come from the same family lineage, difficult to detect which came first, like the chicken and the egg analogy.

In the beginning was vanity, and vanity was with egocentrism...

Regardless of how positive it may be, vanity is always carried in the hands of negative egocentrism.

In our individual nature, egocentrism is always present. The attitudes that distinguish it are pedantry, arrogance, shamelessness, disdain, impertinence, and many others that I would love to enumerate. There may be as many such attitudes as there are numbers.

They come in the same package, "us."

That is what we humans are, an endless set of emotions and attitudes filled with positive vanity and negative egocentrism. Inseparable, they sustain each other; it would be a withered point of our existence to have to rid ourselves of both, since, although vanity may not be indispensable for our mind, it turns out to be an excellent seasoning for the spirit, just like laughter, joy, pleasure, satisfaction, courage, and dedication. I can then say, according to my state of consciousness, that vanity is desirable to have, but it is not necessary to clog the mind with it.

There can be no egocentrism without vanity, nor vanity without egocentrism.

Egocentrism, as negative as it may be, always contains positive reasons to act with pedantry, arrogance, impudence, disdain, impertinence, or other despicable attitudes that may arise. Egocentrism is like a guardian that vigorously fights against foreign ideas or attitudes that are undesirable to our ideal environment. Personally,

I can affirm that seeing it impossible for egocentrism not to affect us, it is inevitable to see fire against fire among the discordant.

Or could a more kind, inclusive, and empathetic guardian be created?

The nature of egocentrism is to disdain, despise, and fight against the undesirable egocentrism of another character; the problem with egocentrism is that it is spread among various individuals and cannot unite through telepathy. Therefore, creating a kind, inclusive, and empathetic egocentrism will be a quixotic task for an unknown period. For now, people will necessarily continue to fight among themselves to resolve their differences. They will use egocentrism even knowing that in the end, everyone lives only a while in miserable and fortunate ways, but then everyone perishes.

Life is just that strange.

The clairvoyant holy eye reveals to me that egocentrism is cruel but necessary, and vanity is vain yet generous. Vanity allows for a certain pride, illusion, and fantasy over some belonging or property while life lasts, even though it may be superficial, empty, or trivial at its core. Vanity is the endorsement of the earthly, the mundane, or the vain as the thrilling essence of existence.

Vanity gives the mind the opportunity to distract itself and fill the void of existence.

Vanity is justice, justice is vanity; vanity is what is needed to agree, to live distracted, to start battles, to die for a cause. Although all may be vain, through the eyes of vanity everything makes sense. There is no need to explain anything because emotions are lived to the fullest when the soul surrenders to its vanity.

Mother of positive emotions

Laughter, joy, pleasure, satisfaction, courage, passion. These positive emotional reactions and all similar ones emerge in those who possess vanity.

Joy = Conformity and pleasure with the vain.
Pleasure = Excitement at obtaining the sensations desired by vanity.
Satisfaction = Compensation for the efforts directed by vanity.
Courage = The boldness of value for the interests of vanity.
Passion = The transmission of energy to the bodies or works of vanity.

Laughter = exaltation of joy caused by a sudden understanding of a personal event; laughter is a sign that there is vanity and egocentrism. The weak laugh out of weakness; the strong laugh out of power. Each laughs according to their property.

Father of negative reactions

Pedantry, arrogance, shamelessness, disdain, impertinence. These negative emotional reactions and other similar ones are born in those who retain egocentrism.

Pedantry = The haughty manifestation of mistreatment towards other egos.
Arrogance = The overloaded sensation of pride when surpassing the abilities of others.
Shamelessness = The daring of an action ignoring the feelings of beings that may be affected.
Disdain = The feeling of contempt for an ego or event not tolerated.
Impertinence = The impulse to interrupt and hinder a dismissed purpose.

The thoughts and emotional reactions of individuals always flutter around the interests of their vanity and egocentrism; however, it is possible for beings to suppress their egocentrism and personality momentarily to enter a broader state of consciousness and meditation.

Deep meditation, unfortunately, will cause both the positive emotions of vanity and the combative reactions of egocentrism to disappear, but only then is it possible to see beyond the current configuration of light.

Chapter 9
Power

The capacity and potential inherent in a body to enact deeds decreed by its own volition is commonly known as power.

Power is of the will; the will is in all life; life is power.

The will manifests when a cluster of matter dedicates itself to performing an action. With this understanding, the entire universe partakes; all that moves, and even that which seems static, is an expression of will.

Every force stems from will; will is the essence of our being.

Macro entities unite with micro entities; inert objects collaborate with mobile ones. Activity is shared and transmitted: the activity of beings aligns with the activity of their cells, the motion of molecules with the motion of their atoms.

> Will interacting with will, will among will, will from the root of will, and will to the power of will.

Programs operate under will; moving objects transmit energy and programming to those that appear immobile. Each program, defined by singular or multiple functions, adheres to a will and intersects with other wills across dimensions.

> The function of the unit echoes the function of its components.

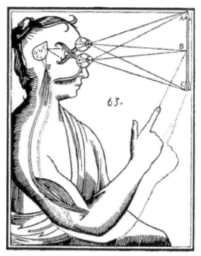

Organs, too, are manifestations of will; thus, beings are constructs of will.

> Every thought is a brainchild of will.

Consciousness and its power

Consciousness is recognized as the entity that grasps knowledge, transforms it, utilizes it, creates or destroys it.

Yet, consciousness recreates itself, crafts beings,
> employs them, and assigns them destinies.

Consciousness consists of memory, free will, and volition that endows it with the power to preserve, cherish, and dictate the fate of matter.

> The universe comprises diverse forms of consciousness and varying expressions of power.

Memory

Every action requires time. Memory is the expanse where time resides, dwelling in the domain of the unconscious; thus, the inception of every action is unconscious.

Time is owned by memory; memory shapes the present, crafts the past, and molds the future.

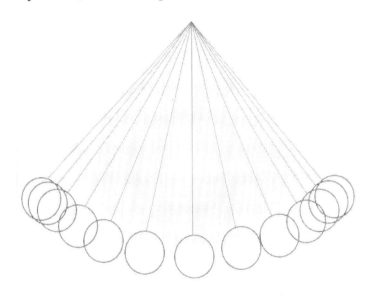

Times oscillate within memory.

The unconscious

The unconscious is the space where all exists. It is antimatter itself, which sustains its counterpart and constitutes all its components, everything consciousness perceives and the entirety beyond itself.

Consciousness inhabits the unconscious.

No memory truly lives or dies; they merely integrate or disintegrate within the unconscious.

The power of space

There are consciousnesses that envelop beings, external memories that serve the grand will which creates and determines their fate.

The memories outside shape the vast cognition of space.

There are consciousnesses whose memory and free will first conceive us, then through their will, endeavor to materialize us. They endow us with memory, free will, and volition, granting us the power to perceive, value, and again dictate the destiny of matter.

Decisions of free will with their own decision
Acts by the will with their own action
Events of memory with their own memories
Creations of cognition with their own power of composition.

The unconscious is the only great memory where multiple individual memories exist. Everything is in memories, and memories are in the unconscious.

The Shift in Power

Memory is periodically cleansed, free will is renewed, and determination timely tests new ideas.

Consciousnesses cyclically renew themselves.

If an act exerted by a certain will is admired and accepted by another will, the possibility and the potency to perform such action spreads to the second will.

Power expands if deemed necessary.

Every consciousness through its free will holds the power to assess the actions it might execute. However, the power to consider an action is not the same as the power to perform the action. The power to execute the act begins with the acceptance of other wills involved in the event where the action takes place. Nonetheless, the independence of wills allows for actions to be taken by certain wills, even though other wills (present at the site of the actions) may disagree. When a power is rejected, accepted, or valued by the consciousnesses that perceive it, new agreements are reached.

When an act is accepted, it is called a right, when it is denied, it is called a wrongful act, when it is committed, it is called an obligation.

Social power

Over time, human minds progress with an idea known as Law, which quickly signifies: the great agreement of wills to regulate society. Currently, the constitution of this idea grants the possibility for some individuals among us to exercise governance.

It is presumed that every human being has rights, is free, and possesses an ego. Moreover, we are all morally endowed with what we call: free will. But this latter is already a social disguise, by convention it was decreed that our will should be free, though practically it is free by nature. It had to be established as a convention because in reality, it is not. We have a prior arrangement that prevents our will from being completely free. This agreement is that upon us exists social power.

The sum of human wills forms social power.

It is understood: social power is an original force among humans necessary to establish an order that maintains our weaknesses safe and curtails freedoms among us. This initial establishment prevents human will from being completely free. In other words, social power limits the autonomy of individuals under the guise of keeping them safe.

Social power naturally acts through decrees such as obligations and prohibitions and institutes agreed-upon terms such as rights and permissions.

The need for agreements among one another consequently creates a system. The organization, self-sustainability, and functioning of a system are reasons that there must be obedience.

Social power represses and permits.

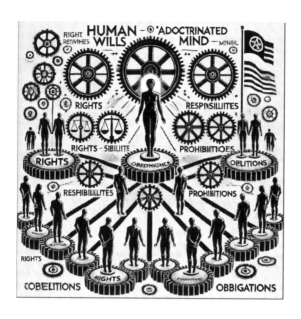

Chapter 10
Obedience

When human wills coalesce, they form a system that includes agreements such as rights, responsibilities, prohibitions, and obligations. A right grants permission for an individual to do something or to obtain something for their benefit (Social authorization). A responsibility imposes a commitment on a person (Duty). A prohibition is a banned power (Wrongful act). And an obligation is a coerced power (A levy).

"Levies" are the most irksome among the system's agreements, as a "coerced act" contradicts the very meaning of the word "agreement." However, a levy is a coerced act accepted as part of the principal agreement of a social system: there must be obedience. The mind that agrees to pay the price of obedience transitions into a state of indoctrinated thinking, its chief achievement being to enter into and preserve some master idea.

The preservation of a sovereign system depends on those who obey.

Those who believe in any sovereignty must recognize their fragility and vulnerability, thus accepting the agreement with like-minded beings around them to stay safe and protected. Dependence is the sole reason for obedience. Giving meaning and sustenance to life in society leads us to the necessity of a deity or a master idea of power.

Principle of authority.

If the power wielded by the authority does not allow for the comfort of its subjects, it will be rejected.

Principle of resistance.

Chapter 11
Resistance

The infamous face of power

Not all agreements of social power are deservedly accepted. However, numerous favored beings, due to the placidity of benefit, no longer dare to question them. These represent the infamous face of power. And this degradation is further reinforced by countless unbenefited beings, who, by the nature of their conformity, lack a voice and also dare not challenge social authority. Thus, we find beings trapped in their unquestioned system, either favored or subdued by the reprimand of power.

If social authority is unchallenged, human intelligence will be dominated.

Social Resistance

Social authority can tighten the interests of the affluent to such an extent that they might lose the sense of freedom they were promised. And when the tributaries of a system begin to feel discomfort with it, they start to take actions to express their discontent. Then, we observe beings representing social resistance, summoning the use of human intelligence to change or modify the agreements that cause upheaval with the system.

As long as there is resistance, we will continue calling for intelligence.

Dirty Power

Since human individuals spend their time seeking agreements with others to generate better living conditions, opportunities constantly arise for one of the parties to create advantageous conditions and benefit more than the other or even at the expense of the other. Dirty power begins when the decrees of an agreement are used to favor only the one who establishes them; sometimes the losing parties cannot deny the contracts due to lack of possibilities. Thus, the winning parties act with treachery and advantage.

Some decrees are set as part of an agreement, but in essence, they constitute the principles of a scam, a win-win for the deceptive party and a lose-or-be-indebted scenario for the trapped party.

The human world is replete with scams signed by the infamous face of power. Those who indifferently enrich themselves at the expense of others cause those who were unjustly harmed based on deceit to also commit wrongful acts and criminal aberrations that feed back into the deterioration of society.

> A dysfunctional society is a creation of dishonest power.

The origin of fraud

The potential for any entity to take action begins with an agreement rooted in free will. Many individuals believe that nature is deceptive, leading them to base their actions and agreements on deceit. Consequently, fraud permeates all levels of society, from the highest to the lowest. It arises from flawed agreements or inadequate deliberations. Nevertheless, because it often yields benefits for the perpetrator, fraud is widely accepted and perpetuated by many.

Fraud becomes contagious when accepted as unavoidable.

The Futile Condemnation of Fraud

"Anyone who in their actions induces others to make a mistake that causes harm is considered a swindler or a fraudster."

Despite the widespread consensus that such behavior is unacceptable, fraud cannot be eliminated simply by labeling it as improper. In the current system, fraud often defends itself and evades accusations, making it not an unthinkable act but rather a very plausible one. Many individuals view fraud as both an object of disdain and a source of desire.

The significant flaw in the system creates opportunities for fraudulent behavior.

Eradicating Fraud

Fraud arises from unjust agreements and flawed social consciousness. Those who engage in fraud are often reacting to a system that imposes excessive hardships. Scammers seek to bypass the restrictions that limit their access to resources. While they acknowledge that others must manage their acquiring power, they refuse to do the same. Fraudsters mock the established order, and as long as the social system remains oppressive, fraud will persist.

To eradicate fraud, it is essential to reform the social power agreements that unduly restrict individual interests.

The Power of Evil

A misguided approach to authority, a lack of understanding of unity, and a misinterpretation of love—all of these elements associated with evil possess the capacity to influence good actions. Without the presence of evil, good would lack a point of reflection.

Ultimately, evil tends to overshadow good.

Evil is not always associated with a lack of understanding or cognitive clumsiness; at times, malice stands in stark contrast to ignorance. The realization that malice can represent a distinct form of order becomes apparent when exploring the depths of a dark, meditative spirit. In its truest form, malice is an unfiltered expression of our nature, unmasked and unafraid of judgment. By rejecting externally imposed notions of good, we discover an inner peace that emerges from acting on our own convictions.

At times, evil may be the most genuine and honest way to exist.

Rebellions

Different organizations will always emerge in rebellion, seeking to challenge established power. Just as fraud resists social authority, malice shatters the constraints of goodness and goodness contemplates the influence of evil. I arrive at the conclusion that rebellions represent alternative forms of power.

An anti-power power.

The Transcendence of Social Power

Social power harbors the ambitious goal of maintaining the sanity of its constituents at the highest level, often at the expense of freedom for anything deemed madness or uncontrolled. However, this approach is not only overly zealous; it is inherently contradictory, as it contradicts the very nature of individuals. Such reprimands lead to lapses where madness, libertinism, and unrestrained enjoyment erupt. By denying these aspects, the world of order devolves into chaos that yearns for joy.

Fun, akin to food and shelter, is essential for human beings.

Social power will only transcend when genuine meditation arises. Within this lies the ability to self-regulate the inherent chaos of freedom and transform it into responsible self-governance for the benefit of the collective to which we all belong.

Chapter 12
Freedom

Beyond the entire construct of light lies true power. Intelligence is born in darkness.

Our existence is a game, a fleeting moment of distraction and recreation. From unconsciousness, we were conceived to become aware of the laws derived from its own evolution. And though we are the fruits of its ordered will, we are also agents of its chaotic imagination. We are the epitome of creation, implanted to achieve recreation and to know satisfaction. All this labor, all these ecosystems, all this construction, all this procreation—for what? What is the purpose of our work and space? We are thus and we are here to enjoy vanity, to cage ourselves in passion, to relish in action. Those who suffer forget they will die, and those who feel they squander forget that all will be lost. We all will depart the same, and those loved ones who leave before us will be remembered even unto our final resting place. We are consciousness and to unconsciousness we shall return, unconscious we were and shall be.

We come to add a bit of chaos to the order that creates us; the unconscious knows that fun only springs from the agreement between the parts. We enter the game when we are aware that there are roles that must be faced to kill boredom. Fun cannot be deprived without the social system exploding. Cyclically, we promote conflicts, but there is no war that does not come for peace; when chaos overwhelms, we tend to restore order. We know how to meditate, erect, and amend the rights and prohibitions that provide each existence with the suitable balance to grow and achieve any action with consideration, granting freedom to our basic needs, including fun. After all, that is our passion: to recreate order and play with chaos to discard boredom.

    Freedom is achieved when unity and resistance have been resolved.

The unconscious allows the partition of reality into multiple and varied existences, represented by different consciousnesses. And a conscious being can still fracture into diverse thoughts. The mind that divides, creates a crossword puzzle of multiple egocentrisms that form the immortal game of lights and shadows, which I have set out to meditate on in these chapters. The resistance and the multiplicity of mechanical powers that govern the pieces play their energy on a mental board of thoughts and feelings. They seek their course, follow their patterns, the unresolved parts resist, they clash with each other, but the reciprocal parts gradually fit together, until finally, the chaos and the course of order are understood.

Finally, the entire game of lights and shadows that disturbs my mind capable of meditation, this entire emotional puzzle, ends. It concludes with the union of all the pieces of the unconscious. I realize that the game is already finished in my mind that reaches the farthest future, oscillates toward the most remote past, and finally returns and stands in the present time. And with my reflective action, I conclude by capturing all the energies of consciousness to facilitate the surrender of my mind to a fully unconscious state.

Since:

Once the light has been turned on, the time has come to turn it off again.

Dark Philosophy
By
Antibuddha.

Made in the USA
Coppell, TX
24 March 2025